The Little
of Storybuilding

by Clêr Lewis and Victoria Millward
Illustrations by Mike Phillips

LITTLE BOOKS WITH **BIG** IDEAS

Published 2013, by Featherstone Education
an imprint of Bloomsbury Publishing Plc
50 Bedford Square, London, WC1B 3DP
www.bloomsbury.com

ISBN 978-1-4081-9416-4

Text © Clêr Lewis and Victoria Millward
Illustrations © Mike Phillips
Cover photographs © Shutterstock

Printed in Great Britain by Latimer Trend & Company Limited

10 9 8 7 6 5 4 3 2 1

This book is produced using paper that is made from wood grown in
managed, sustainable forests. It is natural, renewable and recyclable.
The logging and manufacturing processes conform to the environmental
regulations of the country of origin.

**To see our full range of titles
visit www.bloomsbury.com**

Contents

Introduction

What is Storybuilding?

Communication and literacy lies at the heart of the new Early Years Foundation Stage curriculum (EYFS) and stories are a vital element in learning these skills. In addition to hearing and telling stories, it is important to encourage young children to play and experiment with making group stories. Storybuilding is a co-operative story making process; great for group bonding and for encouraging children to learn and gain confidence from observing and joining in with others.

Storybuilding introduces the basic elements of story-craft (people, place and storyline) in a fun and interactive way and helps children link play and imagination to story structure. Children actively shape their own story with each other's help under the guidance of the adult, so Storybuilding differs from story reading and storytelling but it is a fantastic complement to your setting's range of literacy provision.

Storybuilding is not about creating a perfect story. The value of the process outweighs the end result. It is about encouraging children to share and celebrate creative ideas. A fundamental aspect of Storybuilding is giving the children control when it comes to creating a story. The story is made from their ideas and it is important that even ideas that do not make it into the final story, are still valued and celebrated.

Why is Storybuilding important?

Storybuilding is an incredibly useful tool for helping children enjoy, create and understand stories. It involves play, co-operation and participatory group work, creative thinking, and problem-solving skills and can lead onto a range of related creative arts activities. It is ideal for developing active speaking and listening skills and encourages children to share their ideas and opinions. It is a supportive group task, which strengthens peer relationships and offers a safe way to explore feelings and 'try on' solutions to emotional problems.

Children make decisions and practise choosing the most effective ways to solve whatever problem the story presents to them, developing their confidence and self-esteem. They learn to deal with consequences and can explore boundaries of right and wrong in a safe and supported way. Children are required to make these decisions within the context of a story structure so they gain familiarity with the ingredients of stories, aiding their literacy development.

How do you begin building stories with children?

Adults can work with an individual child or, more often, with a group of children to create an original story from a chosen stimulus. The children's own ideas create the story, making it a very useful child-centred activity.

Stories are developed from a wide range of starting points – observing children at play, popular preoccupations, objects, costume, pictures, sounds and senses, role-play or by taking ownership of an existing story (such as changing the ending, or using the people in the story as characters in a new story). During a Storybuilding session, a story develops fully from scratch to a satisfying conclusion. Follow-on activities can help cement the story theme in the children's mind and help them practise new vocabulary or aspects of story structure, or simply to use the story they have made as a starting point for other creative work.

You know your Storybuilding session is working well when the children are actively contributing ideas. During a good session, many ideas can fly back and forth and the beauty of this activity is that no idea is wrong. I like to think of the adult as the children's Story Guide. It is your job to help the children evaluate which idea is the most useful to move the story forward. You are in role as the connection maker. You have one eye on the end of the story and you guide the group to choose ideas that are most likely to take them to a satisfying conclusion.

Your job as Story Guide is to ask open questions so you can encourage children to problem solve as they create the story together. Open questions are "What if?" questions. This mode of questioning moves the story forward and encourages participation.

> Let's pretend the heroine of your story finds herself surrounded by rising flood waters. If you ask an open question e.g. "What will happen to the heroine?" you allow the children to use the full capacity of their imaginations. Perhaps the children will create a space ship to carry her off, or a giant bird might swoop in to save her, or maybe she'll sink under the water and discover an amazing new watery land. If you ask a closed question e.g. "Where will our heroine find a boat?" you have limited the possibilities of what might happen next in their story.

Encourage children to find solutions through talk and investigation. You can invite them to role-play ideas and draw conclusions as a group. Be observant and make sure you opt for ideas from a range of children. Taking a shy child's idea forward can raise their self-confidence and encourage their future participation.

A beginning, a middle and an end

Always keep in mind the ingredients of stories. You are looking for a beginning, middle and end (or a storyline), an interesting group of people (or characters) and an appealing place where the story takes place (a setting). The middle should ideally involve a problem or conflict that needs to be resolved. Be aware of how much time you have. It is better if the middle moves towards the end without too many red herrings and false turns. If your session is constrained to a strict time limit within the structure of your nursery or school day it can be very frustrating for children to have to stop in the middle because time has run out. At this age it is better to focus on satisfying, well wrapped up endings rather than ambiguous ones – young children like the safety of a satisfying ending.

Of course, inevitably, there will be times when the most impossible to manage idea is desperately championed by the whole group. If everyone loves the crazy idea and you have asked enough open questions for the children to evaluate it, then it is only fair to let the group experiment with using it. Remember it is the children's story at the end of the day, and choosing the impossible ideas can teach a lot about effective use of story structure. Most importantly, you should choose popular ideas which have really caught the children's imagination. This will motivate them to put all their energy and enthusiasm into the story.

As the story develops, re-tell the story a few times to help both you and the children keep track of the storyline. If you forget events, details or names ask the children to help you and I guarantee whatever you have forgotten, they will remember!

It is useful to remember the following list of story ingredients. If you have most of these then the story will unfold to a satisfying conclusion:

- A central problem to solve
- A setting or series of settings
- A beginning, middle and an end
- A mixture of characters – e.g. a goodie and a baddie or a hero and villain
- An obstacle to overcome

There are many ways to develop the story. You can encourage the children to make the story physical using drama and role-play. They can use their facial expressions and body language to portray emotions as well as dramatic movement. Using role-play can encourage children's physical development. It invites children to explore environments physically such as hot, cold, and underwater. Allow children to imagine walking over a rickety rope bridge, crawling into a dark cave, scaling a mountain or being an animal or a monster. You may want to introduce animal or monster noises, if appropriate, but make sure you have set the boundaries beforehand and have a clear signal for when the noise must stop and the bodies must freeze! Using props can also be effective, e.g. a large piece of blue cloth can represent a river and a wooden box can represent a treasure chest.

In order to end the story, the children will need to resolve the conflict or problem or bring the story as near as possible to this. As they practise making stories this will become clearer and easier for them to achieve. It is not necessary to create a perfect story; however, it should be satisfying to the children taking part. After you have created your story, it is a good idea to re-tell it to the group, inviting children to recall the sequence of events.

Before you make a start on the activities in this book, you may find it useful to work through the following step-by-step guide to familiarise yourself with the basic Storybuilding technique.

Step-by-Step Storybuilding:

Step One: Remember, you are the Story Guide and the children are the Storybuilders.

Begin with a group of 4 to 6 children in a quiet area of your setting, as free from distractions as possible. You might say: Today I would like you all to help me build a special story. I would like us to build a story together using all of our ideas. Would you like to help me?

Step Two: Introduce your story inspiration to the group.

This could be an object, a picture, a costume box, a popular character, a storybook etc. There are plenty of ideas for starting stories in the following activity pages but choosing something from the list below to get started, never fails to get children hooked!

▶ a bunch of keys
▶ a ticket
▶ binoculars
▶ a postcard
▶ a necklace or jewel
▶ a cloak

Step Three: Ask open questions about the object to engage the children's imaginations.

Open questions are "What if?" questions. Open questions evoke imaginative thought, encourage response and promote creativity. You might say: What could this object be? Where might you find this object? What does this object do? Does it belong to someone or something? Listen to a range of answers from a variety of children making sure you value and celebrate every idea.

Step Four: Choose an idea to begin your story.

This may be a person or animal the children have suggested or the place where the story takes place. Ensure you have asked enough open questions so you know this place or person well enough to begin. Use story phrasing to indicate to the children that the storytelling has begun. Most commonly, the phrase Once upon a time is used to start a story but you can use any phrase you like.

Step Five: Using ideas from the children, begin telling the story.

Depending upon what the children came up with, you might include: The name and physical description of the person in the story, this person's family or friends, how they feel today, where they live, a description of the setting, the temperature and weather there, any magical or unusual details about the place or person. Continue until you have included all the details you think are useful.

Step Six: Move the story forward.

Remember the story ingredients. You are now moving the story into the middle section of the story. The middle section requires a problem that needs to be solved. Ask open questions to establish the problem that needs to be solved. You might ask: How is the person in our story feeling today? Why? What will help them feel differently? Is today an unusual or special day in this world? You may also ask questions about other people in the story and their relationships, and question further any interesting ideas the children previously mentioned. For example: Why is it raining here? When will it stop raining? Who might be able to make it stop raining?

Step Seven: Continue telling the story by using the children's ideas for the middle section.

Remember to choose ideas that suggest a problem or a journey.

Step Eight: Conclude the story.

The story can end however the children wish. The only rule here is that it is a satisfying conclusion for the group. Do not try to influence the ending if you can. An unfulfilling ending may feel wrong to an experienced storyteller but this is all part of the children's learning process. However, the story must conclude. Beware of suggestions which take the people in your story into a further dilemma or the story will go on all day! Ask open questions that end the action. You might ask, What does the person in our story need to solve this problem? Where will they find this? How will it work? Is there anything else that will stop the person in our story from solving the problem? Do they need help from anything or anyone?

Step Nine: Continue telling the story by using the children's ideas for the ending.

If needed, add a final sentence to round off the story. Familiar end cues are useful such as bedtime, mealtimes, time to pack up, time to go home. You may end the story by saying, After a long day the people in our story yawned, stretched and fell asleep. Alternatively, they were hungry so settled down for a well-deserved feast. They felt glad to be friends again. They knew they would have many more adventures with (the object) but today it was time to go home.

Step Ten: Retell the story.

Don't worry, you won't remember everything. Just try to recall the main events and invite the children to help you remember details and sequence events. It is likely to be a short and simple story but this is perfect when practising the technique.

Links with the EYFS Characteristics of Effective Learning

The Characteristics of Effective Learning support children's learning across all areas of the curriculum. Storybuilding activities are rich with opportunities for children to think, engage and display motivation:

Playing and Exploring

Finding out what they know – showing curiosity about Storybuilding props, the things that happen and the people in the stories, using their senses, engaging in the open-ended story building process.

Playing with what they know – pretending Storybuilding props are things from their experience, representing their experiences through play, taking on a role in their play, and acting out experiences with other people.

Being willing to 'have a go' – showing a 'can do' attitude in response to reaching a particular goal or overcoming a problem in a story, taking risks, engaging in new experiences, and learning by trial and error.

Active learning

Being involved and concentrating – maintaining focus on Storybuilding activities for a period of time, and showing high levels of energy and fascination.

Keeping on trying – persisting with Storybuilding activities when challenges occur, learning that a different approach will pay off, and bouncing back after difficulties arise.

Enjoying achieving what they set out to do – showing satisfaction in meeting the goals and aim of a story, being proud of how their story was built, enjoying the intrinsic rewards of Storybuilding.

Creating and Thinking Critically

Having their own ideas – thinking of ideas and using ideas to overcome problems in a story.

Making links – testing their ideas, and making links and predictions based on their own experiences.

Choosing ways to do things – planning and making decisions about how to develop a story, solving problems and reaching goals, reviewing and changing their ideas as needed.

Links with the EYFS Early Learning Goals

The following Early Learning Goals are relevant to the Storybuilding activities in this book.

PRIME AREAS:

Communication and language

Listening and attention: children listen attentively in a range of situations. They listen to stories, accurately anticipating key events and respond to what they hear with relevant comments, questions or actions. They give their attention to what others say and respond appropriately, while engaged in another activity.

Understanding: children follow instructions involving several ideas or actions. They answer 'how' and 'why' questions about their experiences and in response to stories or events.

Speaking: children express themselves effectively, showing awareness of listeners' needs. They use past, present and future forms accurately when talking about events that have happened or are to happen in the future. They develop their own narratives and explanations by connecting ideas or events.

Physical development

Moving and handling: children show good control and co-ordination in large and small movements. They move confidently in a range of ways, safely negotiating space. They handle equipment and tools effectively, including pencils for writing.

Personal, social and emotional development

Self-confidence and self-awareness: children are confident to try new activities, and say why they like some activities more than others. They are confident to speak in a familiar group, will talk about their ideas, and will choose the resources they need for their chosen activities. They say when they do or don't need help.

Managing feelings and behaviour: children talk about how they and others show feelings, talk about their own and others' behaviour, and its consequences, and know that some behaviour is unacceptable. They work as part of a group or class, and understand and follow the rules. They adjust their behaviour to different situations, and take changes of routine in their stride.

Making relationships: children play co-operatively, taking turns with others. They take account of one another's ideas about how to organise their activity. They show sensitivity to others' needs and feelings, and form positive relationships with adults and other children.

SPECIFIC AREAS

Understanding the world

People and communities: children talk about past and present events in their own lives and in the lives of family members. They know that other children don't always enjoy the same things, and are sensitive to this. They know about similarities and differences between themselves and others, and among families, communities and traditions.

Expressive arts and design

Being imaginative: children use what they have learnt about media and materials in original ways, thinking about uses and purposes. They represent their own ideas, thoughts and feelings through design and technology, art, music, dance, role-play and stories.

Storybuilding from play

Storybuilding from play is a fun and engaging way for practitioners to extend child-initiated play by building an interactive story – the story will be based on the people, places and storylines that the children have independently used in their play.

Group size: small groups of 2-3 children who share a common storyline or narrative in their play, 6-8 children, the entire group

What you need:

▶ post-it notes or observation stickers (for shorter observations) or your setting's long observation format if you are observing a child for a longer period of time

▶ a camera (optional)

▶ a dictaphone or MP3 recorder (optional)

What you do:

1. Trying to keep some distance, observe what children are doing. Without necessarily entering their play, listen carefully to what the children are saying and look closely at what they are doing – listen out for interesting starting points for Storybuilding, e.g. the people, places or storylines that they might be using in their play.

2. Be sensitive when observing – do not be tempted to take over their play, or impose your own ideas! The following tips will support you:

   ▶ Sit on the floor in order to enter the children's world, it will help if you get down to their level.

   ▶ Look carefully at body language, children's actions and the props that they use (e.g. small world figures, costumes etc.). This is particularly important for younger children, or those who don't necessarily talk while they play.

   ▶ Once you have listened and feel 'tuned-in' to what you can see, invite children to tell you more about their play, e.g. by saying, "I really want to know more about this...", or talk about what you can see, e.g. "John is driving a car... brmmm, the car is moving down the road".

   ▶ Show interest by giving your whole attention to what is going on, and show that you are listening by maintaining eye contact, smiling and nodding as they talk to you or play with you – this is where a dictaphone or MP3 recorder can come in really handy!

3. In order for the Storybuilding activity to be engaging and relevant, bring a group of children together to build a story shortly afterwards. Begin by recapping a particular element of what you have observed, e.g. by saying, "Jill has been playing with the elephants this morning", or "Some of you have been building a house to escape from a scary monster!" or "I noticed that there was a birthday party in the home-corner".

4. Remember to respect the children's decisions and choices, but also clarify and guide their ideas in order to build a story. Keep asking open-ended questions!

5. Recap the story, and offer suggestions when children are unsure of how to resolve problems that occur in the storyline, e.g. by suggesting, "Could we try..." or "I wonder what would happen if..."

And another idea:

▶ Make stories through play a regular feature of your daily or weekly routine. Once both practitioners and children become familiar with the process of Storybuilding, you may want to work together to develop a story idea there and then, rather than waiting for group time later on. The children will get a feel for how Storybuilding works, and may start to approach you with their ideas for your next story!

▶ Provide a range of props or costumes relating to a story you have created. At the beginning of the next session remind the children of their previous story and invite them to go on another adventure.

▶ Create a story journal – depending on the age and experience of the children you can use the opportunity to scribe their stories, model writing, or encourage them to 'have a go' at writing a story themselves. Practitioners, parents and carers can then celebrate the children's work by re-telling stories during storytime or whilst in the book corner.

Story trail

Story trails are treasure hunts for stories. They can be used on a visit outside your setting to the park, the shops, the zoo or the seaside where there are lots of unusual sounds and objects to collect. Using your setting's outdoor play area is also a possibility, providing you have enough space for a reasonable trail.

Story trails are all about retelling and recapping stories. This is important when learning about story structure because it helps children learn to sequence events and develop their understanding of how stories are put together. Children's ability to recap and retell events develops the more they do it.

Group size: 4-8 children, the whole group (if during class trip)

What you need:

▶ a bag to carry collected objects
▶ noisemakers and percussion instruments (to use when you return to your setting)
▶ whiteboard and marker/pen and paper
▶ fishing net (optional)

I will need

What you do:

1. During your walk look for good places to stop and ask the children what they can hear, see, smell and touch. Collect objects such as leaves, twigs, pebbles and souvenirs and write down any sounds the children hear e.g. the sound of splashing in puddles, animal sounds, walking in piles of dry leaves or the wind in the trees.

2. When you return to your setting empty out the objects you collected and help the children to put them in the order you found them.

3. If you collected some sounds, talk about when you heard them. Using voice, percussion and noisemakers, try to recreate the sounds you collected. An engaging way to collect sounds is role-playing with a fishing net. Pretend to empty all the sounds out of the net and ask the children to recall where they heard them.

4. With the help of the objects and sounds, invite the children to help you to retell the story of their walk. You can draw a map on the board or on a large piece of paper taped to a table. Ask the children to mark where the 'treasures' and sounds were found as the story unfolds. Invite them to perform the sounds at the appropriate moment and make a rhythm for their footsteps by clapping, body tapping or beating a drum.

5. To help children understand language differences for past, present and future tense, tell the story in the past tense. Ask the children if they would like to go on another Story trail walk in the future. Model language for present, past and future tense:

"We are on a Story trail and we can see..."

"We went on a Story trail and we saw..."

"We are going on a Story trail and we will see..."

And another idea:

▶ Go on a variety of walks to different places. Some could be natural, outdoor environments and some could be around shops or man-made areas.

▶ Add role-play to the Story trail. Ask the children to choose characters to be on the walk – so you may all be explorers, spacemen or deep-sea divers. All the objects and sounds you collect will have new significance as a birdcall becomes a space creature's voice and pebbles become moon rocks!

Storybuilding from objects

In this activity, the children will build a story using a range of objects to prompt the people and places in the story and the storyline. Allow the children to interpret the objects however they wish. If a beach pebble becomes a dinosaur's egg then go with it!

Group size: 4-8 children

What you need:

▶ a tray or a plain coloured piece of fabric

▶ 5-10 objects (depending on the age and experience of the children). Some of the types of objects you might choose:

▷ found objects: feathers, driftwood, shells, pebbles, twigs, tickets, cloth.

▷ pictures: magazine clippings, old photographs, landscapes, paintings.

▷ mail: letters, postcards, parcels, bills, invitations.

▷ familiar and unfamiliar objects: VHS tapes, a trophy, keys, a torch, an old perfume bottle, a Russian doll, jewellery or beads, a camera, coins, a half-burnt candle, a garden trowel, binoculars.

▷ costumes and props: hats, aprons, wands, tails, ears, a basket, capes and cloaks.

▷ food: food packets, napkins, a spoon, a dish, a jar of strong smelling spice such as nutmeg, cinnamon or curry powder.

▷ interpretative objects: a jar of water containing food colouring, silver foil, coloured cellophane.

▷ musical instruments – rain-makers, bells, drums.

▷ toys and puppets.

What you do:

1. Place the objects on the tray or piece of fabric on the floor. We want children to see and consider each object carefully so only offer a small selection. Help the children choose three objects – the first is a clue to where the story takes place, the second is a clue about the people in the story and the third is a clue to what the story is about.

2. Present the objects to the children. Tell them the objects will help them build a story together. Emphasise the importance of making a story together and that everyone's ideas will be heard.

3. Invite a child to come forward and select the first object that will establish where the story takes place. Use open-ended questions to help the children begin to think about the story, such as: "Where is our story happening?" "Can you describe that place... what would you see/smell/hear in this place?"

4. Invite a child to select the second object. This object establishes the main character in the story. If costumes or props have been included let children try them on/try them out. Again, ask open questions to build the main character such as: "Who does this object belong to?" "What is that person's name?" "What do they look like, what do they like to do?"

5. Finally invite a child to select a third object. This object establishes the storyline. This time ask questions that help children think about what might happen in the story. "Why is this object in our story?" "Where is the character going?" "What can they see all around them?" "Who will they meet?" "What do you think might happen next?"

6. Now begin to tell the story by putting the objects in a line where the children can see them. Use the children's ideas to begin telling your story. Continue to ask children for further ideas. Other objects can be used to move the story along if needed.

7. Continue until the story comes to a natural end, the children begin to lose interest, or you are ready to conclude the story.

And another idea:

▶ Try introducing the objects to children with their eyes closed so they can explore each one using their other senses. This can often free up their imaginations and help them to see objects in an abstract or imaginative way.

▶ Use objects that appeal to the senses such as jars of cinnamon or foam balls.

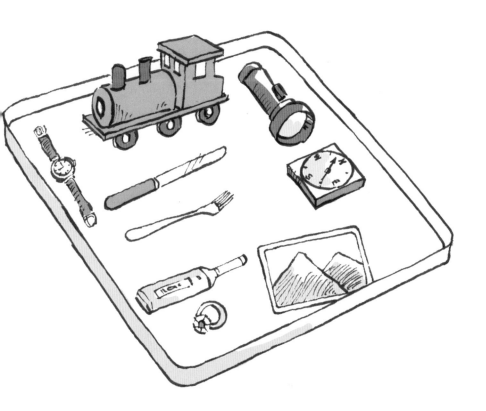

Making a Storybuilding bag

Storybuilding bags are an exciting method of creating stories using objects and they build on the activities already suggested. Storybuilding bags can be purchased from specialist storytelling centres but it is much more exciting to make and fill your own. The Storybuilding bags are for children to collect and store their own Storybuilding objects, but you can make an example yourself that you could use for later activities: Story ingredients in a bag and Storybuilding bags by theme.

Group size: 4-6 children

What you need:

▶ one plain cotton drawstring bag for each child. (You can buy these or make them from cotton fabric or old sheets by cutting out squares and sewing up the sides and top edge. Thread ribbon, string or wool through the fold on the top edge and pull tight to make it into a drawstring bag).

I will need

- a collection of sequins, beads, tassels, pom-poms, glitter glue pens, felt shapes, fabric scraps
- fabric glue and fabric pens
- an iron and ironing board to set the fabric pen to the fabric

What you do:

1. Set up an activity table with a wide range of resources.
2. Tell the children that they will be making Storybuilding bags that need many magic colours and shapes to help them tell as many stories as possible.
3. Use the fabric pens to draw and colour designs. Suggest children use colours that are most magical to them. You could encourage them to draw people and places from favourite stories.
4. Some fabric pens need to be ironed on to set the colour. Follow the instructions for the type you have. If they need ironing now is a good time to set the ink.
5. Glue on a range of sequins, pom-poms and felt shapes. Use self-sticking resources where possible but have some fabric glue on hand just in case extra glue is needed. Children can stick things in rows or patterns. Older children may wish to make flowers, stars or other picture collages on their bags or even to stitch a coloured edging. Help will be needed to thread needles so only attempt this with a small group or older children. Allow all the glue to dry.
6. Once the bags are decorated, invite the children to take them home and collect 'special objects'. Send the bags home with a note for parents/carers about the kinds of objects that the children could collect in their bags, such as: feathers, shells, pebbles, twigs, tickets, fabric, pictures from magazines, photographs, letters, postcards, hats, clean food packets, napkins, a key. Remember to value whatever the children collect in their bags, as just about any object can be used in Storybuilding!

And another idea:

- Encourage children to introduce the objects they have collected in their Storybag to a small group – having engaged with the process of collecting objects for their bags, they will often be motivated to talk about the contents of their bag in front of others. Help the group to build stories using objects collected in the various Storybags.

Storybuilding bag contents

When preparing this activity, try to fill the bags with tactile, brightly coloured and interesting objects. This will capture children's attention and engage their senses, particularly useful for children in your setting who have additional learning needs or whose first language is not English.

You will need three bags to represent each element of your story structure – the place where the story happens, the people (characters) in the story and the storyline.

Children will not be able to see which item they have chosen until it is pulled out of the bag so their imaginations are really tested! Keep an eye on the bags and allow only one object to come out at a time. Children will enjoy playing with and emptying the bags and to start with, give them time to enjoy the excitement of exploring the objects before introducing the story structure.

Group size: 3-7 children so everyone's ideas can be acknowledged and valued. In a larger group it is always best to prepare everyone in advance and explain that not everyone will have a chance to pick something out of the bag.

What you need:

- three cloth drawstring bags. (Decorate them for a more magical appearance.)
- objects for each bag – around 8-10 items per bag

Here are some suggestions for choosing objects:

- **Bag One – the place where the story happens**
  Include found objects like colourful stones, shells, twigs, flowers, a schoolbook, pictures or photographs of places.

- **Bag Two – the characters in the story**
  Include toys like dolls or teddy bears, puppets or objects such as feathers to suggest birds or furry fabric squares to suggest animals. Costume is also fun. Children love trying on hats and easily understand the symbolism of a character they represent.

- **Bag Three – the storyline**
  This bag's contents can represent a journey, a task or an activity. Include toys such as aeroplanes, trains or cars, maps, tickets, postcards, a pair of special flying shoes or a magic carpet, letters, invitations, or familiar and unfamiliar objects such as a wooden spoon or a VHS video tape.

What you do:

1. Settle the children in a quiet area – your story corner or role-play area will work well. Present the bags to the children as 'Magic Story Bags' that contain a story. Ask them to help you build their special story from what is hidden inside the bags.

2. Start with Bag One – the place where the story happens. Invite a child to pull something out of the bag to start your story. Ask questions about the object until there is a group consensus about where the story will take place. You will referee the ideas making sure to celebrate them all: "Where is our story happening?" "Can you describe that place?" "Imagine you are there – what can you see?"

3. Now suggest to the children that you need to discover the main character in the story. Present Bag Two – the characters in the story. Invite a child to pull an object out of it. Ask questions to create your characters: "What is this character's name?" "What do they like/dislike?" "What do they look like?" "How old are they?" "Who might this object belong to?" "Who might use this object in their work?"

4. Now present Bag Three – the storyline. This bag's contents offers a clue about what might happen to the main character or the journey they need to make. Ask questions to establish what is going to happen in this story: "Why is this object in our story?" "Is the character going to take the object somewhere?" "Why?" "What can they see all around them?" "Who will they meet?" "What do you think might happen next?"

5. Display the chosen objects and begin telling the story using the ideas the children have put forward. It can be useful to use story phrasing such as "Once upon a time" to indicate to the children that the story has started. Some stories can be very simple and others might require multiple dips into the story bags to source various characters, places and activities. Recap the story as you go to refresh your memory and the children's. It helps them keep track of all the ideas and to recall and order information.

6. Using the chosen objects, encourage the children to help you retell the story to the rest of the group.

And another idea:

▶ If you are working with the same group of children, keep changing the objects in the bags so new things keep coming out.

▶ Try recalling the story through role-play with children taking on the roles of the characters. Take photos of the children acting key parts of the story – encourage the children to sequence the images when retelling their story.

▶ Fill the bags with objects which match your setting's current wider theme e.g. under the sea, outer space, friendship.

Storybuilding bags by theme

A Storybuilding bag is a simple way to organise objects by theme. They are also useful for retaining a group of objects so themes can be revisited again later without investing more time sourcing and gathering objects. In this activity, children are introduced to a new topic in a fun and interesting way. You could also use it to reinforce or assess what children have remembered about a theme previously explored.

roup size: 4-8 children, larger groups (experienced)

What you need:

▶ a story bag
▶ a collection of 5-8 objects related to a chosen theme or topic.
  Use more objects for older or more experienced children.

  Some examples to get you started are:

The Seaside:

▷ a piece of driftwood
▷ a bucket and spade
▷ a screw top jar full of water and food colouring
▷ a shell
▷ a piece of blue cloth
▷ sand

Shopping:

▷ a shopping bag or basket
▷ an unfinished shopping list or a recipe
▷ some fresh fruit and vegetables
▷ a purse with some coins in it
▷ food packets
▷ a receipt

A Celebration:

▷ indian sari or cloth
▷ Diwali lamps or clay divas
▷ CD of Bhangra music
▷ Rangoli patterns on cards
▷ recipes for Indian sweets
▷ picture card of Lakshmi

What you do:

1. Gather the children in a quiet area and present the
   Storybuilding bag to them. Tell them the bag contains a story
   and they must try to guess what the story will be about.

2. Invite a child to pull out an object. Ask some open questions about the object:
   "What type of object is this?" "Where might you find this object and when?"
   "Who would own an object like this?" "What could it be used for?"

Children may need 2-3 objects before they see a pattern and guess the theme. If it's a familiar topic ask children to recall what they already know about this theme. Go back through the objects to investigate further.

Ask the children: "Does this give us a clue about the other objects? Who may need all these things?"

Look out for useful suggestions for where the story takes place, the people in the story and the storyline. Retell the ideas that fit well together and ask the children: "Are we ready to tell the story?" You should have around five objects to work with.

Begin building the story. Continue introducing new objects from the bag until the story comes to a natural end, the children begin to lose interest, or you are ready to conclude the story.

And another idea:

▶ Include foods that children could taste in the bags such as Indian sweets for Diwali (do check first for any children who have food allergies).

▶ Introduce role-play into the story. You could try:
   ▷ inviting children to try on a costume and walk, stand or talk in character
   ▷ inviting children to dance or move to related music such as Bhangra
   ▷ exploring emotion faces and body language e.g. anger, surprise, fear

▶ Leave the objects out for children to independently revisit the story they have made or to make up new stories.

Storybuilding a journey

A journey is a great idea for a story because it offers so many opportunities for an exciting adventure and the possibility of meeting interesting characters. In this activity, the use of objects like maps, tickets and luggage really get children thinking about travel and expeditions. If you link this activity to a wider topic, it provides a starting point for learning about transport and other countries and cultures.

Group size: 3-8 children

What you need:

- a suitcase – an old brown leather type with lots of wear and tear and travel stickers would be ideal to get the imagination flowing! You could also use a backpack, holdall or a child's suitcase.
- a selection of objects for a journey, voyage or expedition:
  ▷ tickets and maps
  ▷ binoculars or telescope
  ▷ travel pillow
  ▷ a packed lunch
  ▷ a passport
  ▷ a sea captain or airplane pilot's hat (or other appropriate costume)
  ▷ objects indicative of a setting – small world figures, found objects such as driftwood or shells
  ▷ fruit or food indicative of particular countries or environments, e.g. coconuts, bananas, curry powder
  ▷ pictures of settings or landscapes – paintings, postcards, magazine clippings

What you do:

Tell the children you have a very special suitcase that contains a story just for them. Invite them to help you build the special story. Sit together and put the case or bag in the middle of the group so all the children can see it.

Before you open the case or bag, talk about journeys. "What is a journey?" "You go on a journey to school/nursery each day... why else might we take a journey?" (e.g. to the shops, to visit your family, to the park). "How do you travel?" (e.g. walk, bus, car, bike). "Have you been to another country?" "How did you travel on that journey?"

Open the case or bag. Invite children to select items – one for the people, one for the start of the journey, one for the end of the journey, one for how the people will travel and one for the reason for the journey. Ask open questions about each selection. "Who does this object belong to?" "Where do they live?" "Where do you think they will travel to?" "How will they make their journey?" "Why are they going on a journey?"

When the children have selected all the required items, line them up where children can see them and use their ideas to begin telling your story. Continue to ask children for further ideas as the story builds. Go on until the story reaches the journey's end.

5. Invite the children to share or act out their journey to the rest of the group, helping them to recall and retell the events in the correct order.

And another idea:

▶ Encourage children to draw the destination from their journey or make a collage picture using tickets, maps, luggage labels.

▶ Introduce suitcases, rucksacks or trunks into your role-play area so children can role-play journeys or consider building a role-play area that relates to travel, e.g. a bus or a train station – whatever your children have had direct experience of outside of school.

▶ Talk about journeys to new countries. Some children may have strong links to their countries of origin so it may be appropriate to take a story journey to a particular country or region. You could use this activity to explore topics about migration. Some children may have migrated as refugees or asylum seekers so be sure the topic is explored sensitively. The Paddington Bear picture books by Michael Bond provide an accessible story context for exploring why people move to different countries.

Story hunt

This activity helps children learn about story ingredients – people, place and storyline. It is the ideal follow-on from Storybuilding bags or Storybuilding from objects so children are used to using objects for building stories before they take it into a new environment.

Group size: 4-5 children

What you need:

▶ an object to represent a possible character e.g. costumes, dolls, teddy bears, small world figures, puppets, feathers (to suggest birds), furry fabric squares (to suggest animals).

▶ an object to represent a place – pebbles, twigs, flowers, a library book, a coin book or even pictures or photographs of a famous place.

▶ an object to represent the story line e.g. toy aeroplanes, trains or cars, maps, tickets, postcards, a magic flying carpet, letters, invitations, or everyday objects such as a wooden spoon.

▶ an object to represent an ending e.g. a door key suggesting time to go home, a dinner plate suggesting time for tea or a blanket suggesting time for bed.

▶ brightly coloured wrapping paper or tissue paper

What you do:

1. Wrap the objects up in brightly coloured wrapping paper or tissue paper.

2. Hide your chosen objects where you would like the story hunt to take place. Choose interesting, evenly spaced positions that are not too close to each other. The first three objects can be found in any order.

3. Tell the children that you are going on a Storybuilding adventure and that nobody knows what the story is going to be. Ask the children to help you find the magic ingredients that will tell the story – the characters, the place, the storyline and the ending. Show the children the wrapping paper and explain the magic objects will be wrapped up in this paper.

4. Suggest where the children should begin to look for the first clue – the character object. When it is found, unwrap the object together. Start the Storybuilding process by asking open questions. Some starting points you may find useful to ask about a character are: "What is this character's name?" "What would they like to do?" "Dislike?" "What do they look like?" "Who might own this object?" "Who might use this object?"

5. When you have talked about and agreed on the main character of the story, move to object two, which is a clue to the place or setting. Celebrate when the object is found so the children invest in the value of the game. Often children will pick up other objects in their excitement to be the one who finds the hidden object. Acknowledge that this object could make a great addition to another story but remind them the object you need for this story is wrapped in the special paper.

Ask questions about the object to establish the place or setting: "Where is our story happening?" "Can you describe that place?" "Imagine you are there – what can you see?"

Recall the information you have so far before suggesting the children look for the third object. When you have recapped, look for the third object – the storyline. Ask questions about the object to establish what may happen in the story. "Why is this object in our story?" "Is the character going to take the object somewhere?" "Why? "What can they see all around them?" "Who will they meet?" "What do you think might happen next?"

Begin building the story using the suggestions the children have made. When you near the end of the story, remind the children there is one final object to find in order to discover how the story ends!

When they have found the fourth and final object, discuss how this might end the story. Retell the story and add the ending.

And another idea:

▶ Ask the children to bring objects from home – remember which child has contributed which object! These objects can then be used to make a new story hunt.

▶ Record the stories in a book to display in the book corner or on a MP3 player for children to listen to in the reading area or during a storytime session.

▶ Help the children to act out the story, encouraging them to explore a range of movements whilst retelling the story.

Magical me!

This activity helps children to invent characters to use in Storybuilding, inspired by their own likes and preoccupations.

Group size: 3-6 children

What you need:

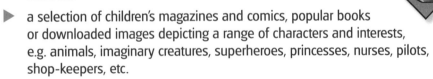

▶ floor space large enough for a group of up to 6 children to work on.

▶ a selection of children's magazines and comics, popular books or downloaded images depicting a range of characters and interests, e.g. animals, imaginary creatures, superheroes, princesses, nurses, pilots, shop-keepers, etc.

▶ a roll of paper or piece of sugar paper large enough to draw around a child's body, masking tape, chunky pens or crayons.

What you do:

1. Secure the paper to your floor space, and have appropriate drawing and mark making materials ready.

2. Provide children with the opportunity to independently explore and discuss their likes and preoccupations and their favourite characters from stories and TV – introduce this theme at the beginning of the session and make images available for children to look at throughout.

3. Invite a group of children to sit on the floor around the large piece of paper.

4. Explain to the children that they are going to invent a character of their own. Draw around a child's body so that you have a life-sized outline. Asking the following key questions, invite children to decide what their character will look like, and what they are able to do such as any magic powers or their occupation: "What would Magical Me wear on this part of its body?" "Why?" "Does anybody know whether Magical Me has any special powers?" "If we were to draw that power, what might it look like?" "Is there anything strange or interesting about this part of its body?" "How is Magical Me similar to/different from your favourite TV or storybook character?" As the character is created, you and the children can take turns drawing and colouring in the character.

5. Once finished, cut out the drawing – children will enjoy and benefit from having the opportunity to introduce their character to other children in the group. Agree with the children where the character will live, and display him/her accordingly, perhaps in the book corner, home corner or role-play area.

And another idea:

▶ Whilst observing and playing alongside the children, use their characters as the basis for building stories. Ask the children: "Does your character have a name?" "What would they like to do today?" "Where are they going?" "What can they see all around them?" "Who will they meet?" "What do you think might happen next?"

▶ Provide large-scale paper for children to work on independently to create more characters, or smaller photocopied paper outlines of a body on which they can individually record their ideas.

▶ Help the children to draw around their bodies with chalk (perhaps onto a wall in the outdoor area). They can then work together to create and draw a character's feature onto the outline.

Storybuilding from music

This activity uses music as a stimulus for exploring story places or settings. We all 'see' or feel something unique when we listen to a piece of music – this provides fantastic scope for helping children to imagine story places. Children will be able to apply the listening skills they acquire through this activity in many other areas of learning.

Group size: 3-6 children. Once children understand the expectations for the activity and for older more mature children, it can be done with larger groups.

What you need:

> a clip of around 60 seconds of a piece of unfamiliar music – it is important that you avoid popular music or pieces of familiar music that children will associate with particular experiences or visual images. Choose music that will engage the children's imaginations – does it contain a range of sounds? Silence? Loud or quiet sounds?

Classical or World music works well. Some examples are:

▷ Peer Gynt – Edvard Grieg

▷ Nutcracker Suite – Tchaikovsky

▷ The Carnival of the Animals – Saint Saens

▷ The Flight of the Bumblebee – Rimsky Korsokov

▷ Peter and the Wolf – Prokofiev

▷ Rough Guide to World Music for Children

▷ Putomayo Presents – World music for children e.g. Instrumental Dreamland, Gypsy Groove, India, Celtic Tides, Arabic Beat

> a CD or MP3 player

> a quiet space so children will be able to hear the music easily. If you have a listening post and headphones, you could use these.

> a rug or cushions so that children feel relaxed enough to engage with the activity.

What you do:

Before you start, set up your listening area. Remember to limit the selection of music you play to around 60 seconds so the children can retain their focus and so you can re-play the music without the activity becoming too long.

Invite children to the listening area, explaining that they are going on a 'listening journey'. It is a good idea to agree on rules for listening, e.g. Relax your body, be still and quiet, close your eyes, etc. Perhaps count down from 5 before playing the music.

Asking the following questions, invite children to think about and articulate what they saw or imagined while they were listening: "While you were listening, did you go on a journey?" "What could you see?" "Could you describe for us..." "How did you feel?" "Why?" "Tell me more about..."

4. Recap the range of ideas that children have come up with, before listening to your music again: "I'd like to know if you saw something you didn't notice last time, or perhaps you saw something very different?"

5. If relevant, listen again and help children to add details to the place they have imagined. Don't worry if children all latch on to the same idea or repeat the same ideas each time they listen to a different piece of music. This in itself is valuable as it may reveal a child's pre-occupations with a particular theme or a group's interests that can then provide the basis for a topic or a new context for engaging them.

6. Discuss the kinds of stories that could happen in the places they imagined.

And another idea:

▶ Provide resources for children to draw their imagined places and story worlds. Allow time for children to describe and compare their ideas with each other. Their drawings can be displayed in the book corner, role-play area or as a backdrop to a puppet theatre. Adults can encourage children to travel to their imagined places during role-play and Storybuilding activities.

▶ If you wish to explore a particular environment that links to your topic, you can channel the children's imaginations by finding a piece of music that you think links well. Explain that you are going on a listening journey to, e.g. the jungle, the shops, or under the sea – this can be very useful at the beginning of a topic in order to ascertain children's prior knowledge and understanding of a particular environment.

Storybuilding with water play

In this activity, children will learn more about the everyday task of washing and laundry and will have the opportunity to talk about their own experiences of using water such as bathing and showering or keeping things clean at home.

Group size: 2-6 children

What you need:

- a water tray or large bowl or bucket filled with warm water
- bubble bath and plastic cups, funnels, jugs, water spray bottles and scrubbing brushes
- towels and aprons
- a small plastic toy, such as a dog or a doll

What you do:

1. Begin the session by letting the children explore the water independently. Using the water tray or water containers, invite the children to put their hands in the water, to add bubble bath and to experiment with collecting and pouring water into different containers. If you do not have a suitable area for water play, another option is to spray water onto the hands and feet of children using a water spray bottle. Allow children at least ten minutes to play in the water before you dry off.

2. Ask the children to describe the water and the bubbles. Encourage the use of words such as drip, bubble, gurgle, swish, whoosh, splash, pop, glisten, sparkle.

3. Introduce the children to the plastic toy. Show them that the toy is dirty and needs a wash. "Let's build a story to help the toy get clean!"

4. Ask open questions about the toy: "What's his name?" "Who does he belong to?" "How did he get so dirty?" "How does he feel?"

5. Begin telling the story using the children's ideas about the toy and why he needs a wash.

6. Ask open questions about how to help the toy get clean: "How do we wash ourselves at home?" (bath and shower, sponge, soap, shower gel, bubble bath) "How do we wash our clothes?" (laundry, washing machine, washing powder, spin) "What else do we wash at home?" (floors, windows, pets, bucket, cloth) "How does the toy get clean in our story?" "What does he like or dislike?" "How does he feel afterwards?"

7. Now, let the children have fun washing the toy(s).

8. Once you have finished the activity, sit the children down in a quiet (dry!) area and retell the story. Ask the children to recall some of the words they used earlier for describing water and bubbles. Use these words while retelling the story. How does the toy look now that he is clean? (dazzling, bright, spic and span, fresh, shiny, good as new).

And another idea:

▶ Set up a laundry area for children to role-play washing dolls clothes. Include a washing line so the clothes can be pegged out to dry. You could also include plastic tea sets so children can role-play washing dishes.

Costumes on a washing line

Dressing up is a great way for children to develop their imaginations and their experimental and fantasy play. It is also a good way to take an in-depth look at people and animals in stories including stock characters such as 'the goodie' or 'the baddie', the witch, the princess, the soldier, the doctor, etc. This activity helps children to explore a range of characters that they can use in their Storybuilding.

Group size: 6-8 children

What you need:

▶ a washing line or piece of string tied securely between two points

▶ enough clothes pegs to hang up all the costume items

▶ a camera, sticky labels and pens

▶ between 10-12 costume items depending upon the age and experience of the children. There is a place for valuing children's favourite story figures but for this activity it works better if your costume choices are generic and open to interpretation. This gets children using their imaginations to construct their own characters.

Some suggestions for costume are:

▷ ears, tails, furry fabric to use as animal capes

▷ a range of hats for stock characters – witch, chef, policeman, fireman, doctor or nurse, astronaut helmet, crown or tiara

▷ cloaks – a range of colours, animal print or shiny and metallic fabric

▷ an apron

▷ woolly hat, mittens and scarf or sunglasses and sun hat

▷ masks

▷ feather boa

▷ tool belt

▷ necklaces and bangles

▷ culturally relevant costumes such as African cloth, Indian sari fabric and traditional dress from other countries and cultures

What you do:

1. Gather the children together. Place all the costume items and clothing in the centre of the circle and tell the children you need their help to create some characters for Storybuilding.

2. Invite one child to come forward and pick a piece of clothing from the pile and to put it on.

3. Ask open questions about who might wear this: "Could this character be an animal or a person?" "What do they look like?" "Do they live somewhere hot or cold?" "What's their name?" "How old are they?" "Are they rich or are they poor?"

4. Ask the children: "Is there anything else in the circle that this character might like to wear?" Continue until the child is wearing two or three items of costume that suggest something about the character and how they live.

5. Ask the children: "How does this character feel?" "Are they feeling happy or sad?" "Are they angry or upset or worried?" "Using our bodies and faces, how can we show that we feel angry or sad or happy?"

6. Repeat this process until you have made four or five characters, inviting a different child each time to model the costume.

7. Ask the children to tell you how all these characters know each other: "Do these characters all live in the same place?" "Are they friends with each other?" "Are they in the same family?" "How did they meet each other?"

8. Peg all the costumes onto the washing line and label each costume with the character's name. Older or more experienced children may like to write labels or make marks by themselves. Encourage the children to have a look in the dressing-up box, asking: "Can you make up another character?"

And another idea:

▶ Print photos of the children in character and display them near the washing line. Remember to celebrate the various characters the children invent by taking additional photos for the display.

▶ Help the children to make simple pieces of additional costume such as headbands, tabards or paper cloaks to represent the characters they have created.

Making a magic story carpet

Here we are using a felting technique to make a magic carpet, which will then be used as the inspiration for building story journeys. Felting is a wonderfully tactile activity and is particularly appealing to children with sensory impairments.

Caution!
Take care to check for children with detergent allergies before you begin. Rubber gloves can be worn for this activity but feeling the warm bubbles between your fingers should not be missed where possible. For children with allergies to detergent, gloves are an option or use hand soap or shampoo on their section of the carpet.

Group size: 3-6 children

What you need:

- coloured wool tops
- two large pieces of calico cloth
- washing up liquid (or shampoo or soap)
- a container holding warm water
- a container holding cold water
- a sink area with running water facilities near to the activity
- a washing line for drying the felt
- rubber gloves for children with allergies
- aprons
- a suitable area for this wet and messy activity to take place (ideal outdoor activity if not too windy!)

What you do:

1. Lay one piece of calico cloth across a table and invite the children to stand around the cloth. Explain that you are going to make a magic carpet from the coloured wool tops. You can use a prop like a magic wand or say a magic rhyme or spell to change the wool into a 'magic story carpet'. Explain that you will know the spell has worked if the wool changes from separate strands into a solid carpet.

2. Wool tops are pieces of wool that have been cleaned, carded and dyed. The next stage of the wool making process would be to spin the wool into yarn but for this activity, we want to use the fluffy wool as it is. Invite the children to choose some handfuls in different colours that they think best fit a 'magic story carpet'.

3. Gently separate the wool into thin strands and lay them on the calico. It is very important that everyone lays the wool strands in the same direction. Begin laying them in a horizontal direction.

4. When you have covered the calico, begin another layer on top. This time you must lay the strands in a vertical direction. This mimics the warp and weft of woven cloth and will enable the wool to stick together firmly.

5. Continue laying out the wool in this pattern until you have the thickness you desire. As a minimum have two layers horizontal and two layers vertical but the thicker the better.

6. Now lay the second piece of calico over the wool and press it down taking care not to disturb the wool beneath.

47

7. Carefully wet the entire calico cloth with warm water. Don't add too much water. You want just enough water to run through the top layer of calico and through the wool. Now squirt a little washing up liquid over the cloth and invite the children to rub the cloth and make as many bubbles as they can.

> **Caution!**
> Water and soap will spill onto the floor in this activity so take some time to talk to the children about safety. They should be told to walk carefully as the floor may be slippery and listen carefully to instructions when adults are handling warm water containers.

8. You may want to introduce some songs here or play around with rhythms. Also try circling your hands around and moving them up and down or backwards and forwards. This activity is wonderful for children with physical disabilities as it very sensory and really gets fingers and hands working. When you have rubbed one side for a good 10 minutes, turn the cloth over and rub the other side. Continue turning backwards and forwards until tiny flecks of wool start to appear through the calico. This tells you the wool has fused.

9. Plunge the calico and wool structure first into very hot water. Allow to rest for 2 minutes. Then plunge into cold water and allow to rest for 2 minutes. Wring out as much water as you can.

10. Invite the children to say the magic spell together or use your wand prop. Carefully peel away the top layer of calico. Underneath you should find a multi-coloured felt piece of fabric. Remove the rest of the calico. The carpet may need another few rinses to get rid of the soap but make sure to do a final cold water rinse to shrink the fibres into place. Hang on the line to dry.

11. When the carpet has dried it is ready for use as a 'magic story carpet' and it's first Storybuilding journey!

And another idea:

▶ Make a rainbow carpet by laying white wool tops on the bottom and rows of individual colours on top.

▶ Children can make individual pictures on a small square of calico inspired by a favourite story or character. They can then be displayed or patch-worked together to make carpet.

Magic carpet journeys

Magic carpet journeys use drama and guided role-play to build interactive stories. Children and practitioners work in character to bring a story world to life. Children can decide where their imaginary journey will take them and what they will see and experience or practitioners can lead the activity to fit with a current topic.

Group size: 4-8 children

What you need:

➤ a magic carpet! This can simply be a piece of fabric, a throw or a small rug or carpet off cut. Alternatively you could make a 'magic carpet' (see previous activity)

➤ props and/or atmospheric music (optional)

I will need

What you do:

1. Invite the children to sit in a circle on the 'magic carpet'. Spend some time talking to them about what a magic carpet can do and where it might go. Invite them to share a journey on this carpet with you.

2. Ask the children what they think they need to take with them on a journey. Remind them of a school trip or family outing and ask them to recall what things were needed then. Some suggestions may be: a packed lunch, a raincoat, a torch, a sunhat, a telescope. With each suggestion, ask the children to mime placing that object in their imaginary rucksack. You could take the opportunity here to practise memory skills by re-listing all the objects that they packed.

3. A magic carpet needs a special spell to work. Invite the children to share any magical or favourite words they know. Made-up words are perfectly acceptable here. Say the spell all together and role-play the carpet beginning to rise. Including a movement, a rhythm or holding hands can help shy children feel involved.

4. Ask the children what they can see, hear and smell as the carpet speeds along. Suggestions may be: clouds, birds, raindrops, stars, aeroplanes. Ask them to look out for an interesting place to land. Suggestions are: other countries, a castle, a forest, the North Pole.

5. When you have chosen a suitable place to land, bring the carpet to earth. It is time to explore the surroundings. Ask the children what treasures they expect to find in a land like this and either as a group or as individuals invite them to explore the land and role-play bringing back a treasure. Remind them the carpet only lands for 10 minutes so they must rush back when you call them.

6. Ask each child to hold up their imaginary object and describe it. Then ask them to carefully put their treasure in their imaginary rucksack.

7. When you are ready to leave, say the magic flying rhyme again and role-play the carpet rising. Ask them to tell you what they can see on their journey home. You can invite children to use imaginary telescopes to see into the distance. Ask them to look out for home so you can land safely. Encourage them to describe what the earth and your nursery setting looks like from above.

8. Try recalling and retelling the adventure as a group. This will help children's ability to sequence stories. Children who have learned to sequence events will find it easier to produce good written work as they progress through their education.

And another idea:

▶ Think of other journeys you could try. Can you link them to current topics such as outer space, under the sea, or the jungle? Suggest to the children that the carpet takes you to one of these locations.

▶ Try using props to add to the atmosphere. If you are going to the moon for example, a simple tin foil hat can help children get into role or some magic goggles can be a useful prop for under water journeys. You could make and decorate telescopes out of paper or cardboard tubes to take with you on your next journey.

▶ Sound effects and music could be used to add to the journey. You may choose to play the same music everytime the carpet is flying. Invite the children to lie down as the clouds sweep past overhead. As the soothing music plays ask them what shapes the clouds are making today.

Making a puppet theatre

Puppet theatres encourage children to use their imaginations to build their own stories using simple character puppets. If your setting does not have a puppet theatre, they are very quick and easy to make using a plain cardboard box.

Group size: 2-5 children to create the theatre, or prepare it in advance and invite the children to add the scenery

What you need:

- a large cardboard box
- scissors or a craft knife
- packing tape
- a roll of black paper
- glue and brushes
- black card (optional)
- red paper
- drawing paper and colouring pens, pencils or crayons
- blu-tack

What you do:

These instructions are for a puppet theatre that is accessed from underneath – much like a traditional Punch and Judy box.

1. Identify the opening flaps of the box. These are the four pieces of cardboard usually used to close the box. Keep the two large ones intact and cut off the smaller ones. These are now the curtains for your puppet theatre. (If your box doesn't have these flaps then cut down the middle of one side and bend the card flaps back).

2. Using the packing tape, seal all the other edges of the box to make sure the box is completely closed and all seams are sturdy.

3. Cut a rectangle piece out of the bottom of the box. This is the hole the child's hand will come through when holding their puppets. Make sure it is big enough to fit a hand.

4. Using the black paper, cover the outside and inside of the box and stick it down with glue.

5. Using the red paper, cover the flaps you left free for the curtains.

6. Use the black card to cut out a decorative edging to sit on the top front edge of the box above the curtains. Stick this on with glue.

7. Invite the children to draw a picture such as a landscape as scenery. Attach the scenery inside the box to the back wall of the theatre with blu-tack. By using blu-tack you can keep changing the setting to make it relevant to the story the children are building.

8. Use the theatre to re-enact stories you have created in your Storybuilding sessions.

And another idea:

▶ Try using different sized boxes. A shoebox theatre is a nice size if you want everyone in your group to have a go. Make it in the same way as described above but on a smaller scale.

▶ Take your group to see a puppet show. There are many age appropriate productions which will give the children plenty of ideas and inspiration to work with back in the setting.

▶ Use the puppet theatre to act out a story at storytime instead of reading from a book. You can include the children by asking them to manipulate the puppets for you while you tell the story.

Making a simple character puppet

Puppets are an appealing way to explore a Storybuilding world and offer a good 'way in' for shy children who need a little prompting when it comes to role-play. Puppets can be made very quickly and easily using simple and readily available resources such as wooden spoons, paper plates, paper bags or woollen gloves. Spending some time creating a puppet making kit will allow children the freedom to respond spontaneously to any Storybuilding world they are creating.

Group size: 2-8 children; larger groups

What you need:

▶ a table suitable for sticking and gluing activities

▶ wooden spoons

▶ a puppet making kit which includes masking tape and felt-tip colouring pens along with a variety of ribbons, trim, sequins, pom-poms, fabric scraps, glitter glue, wool, lace, pipe-cleaners, etc.

What you do:

1. After introducing children to the resources, tools and techniques that can be used to make a puppet, children can engage independently with this activity. It may be useful to set this activity up in the role-play corner if you have created a Storybuilding world, or near your puppet theatre.

2. Observe children interacting and playing in the Storybuilding world or with the puppet theatre. Note the characters they are creating.

3. Allow them to complete their play before you interact. Ask them about the character they have created: "What do they look like?" "What is their name?" "Age?" "Where do they live?" "What colour are they or are their clothes?" "Do they have hair?" "Are they happy/sad?" "What are they wearing today?"

4. Invite the children to make a wooden spoon puppet of their character. They may need some help and encouragement the first time they try this. Model drawing the face on the bowl of the spoon, wrapping pipe-cleaners around the stem for the arms and attaching the clothes, scales or fur with masking tape.

5. Make children aware that the puppet making table is set up for them to use whenever they want to make a character puppet to use in their role-play or Storybuilding.

6. Display some of the wooden spoon puppets in your setting so other children have a model to use as inspiration.

And another idea:

▶ Introduce the children to other types of puppet making materials. Instead of spoons you can use gloves, paper plates, paper bags, toilet roll tubes or cereal packets.

▶ Help the children to create a range of puppets that link to your topic. Store the puppets invitingly in a basket next to the puppet theatre and encourage the children to use them independently in their Storybuilding.

Storybuilding worlds – Under the sea

Storybuilding is a great way to explore themes and topics. You can encourage children to include facts and information they have learned about a topic in their stories, or you can use Storybuilding to introduce a brand new topic in a fun and exciting way.

In this activity, children will explore an underwater Storybuilding world through role-play, mime and imaginative play. This technique can be used to introduce many different topics such as: the jungle, the shopping centre, train stations, parks, the doctor's surgery, the post office, snowy places, hot places, etc.

roup size: 4-8 children; larger groups

What you need:

▶ a large piece of blue cloth about the size of a bed sheet. Try to use a light fabric – satin, chiffon or silky fabrics are best.

▶ a clean pair of goggles or a snorkelling mask

▶ a bubble gun or bottle of bubbles and bubble wands

What you do:

1. Invite children to sit in a circle around the blue cloth. Tell the children the cloth is the ocean and today they are going to join you in building a story about life under water.

2. Begin by telling the children they are the wind. Start by blowing the fabric to see if you can make it ripple. Then ask everyone to hold the fabric around the edges and try wafting the fabric to create waves and ripples.

3. Tell the children you have a magic pair of goggles – whoever wears them can see under the water, all the way down to the bottom of the sea. In turn, each child will put on the goggles and look under the blue cloth. Ask them to share what they can see at the bottom of the sea. Examples you can prompt with are fish, crabs, mermaids, rocks, seaweed, eels, sharks, lobsters, a submarine, an oyster. Get as much information about what they imagine about life under water as possible to make the story world really come to life: "What colour are the fish?" "What do mermaids look like?" "Use describing words to tell me about what you can see"

4. Tell the children that they are deep-sea divers. Invite them to mime swimming under water using the cloth as the stage. You can use a bubble gun to blow bubbles to add atmosphere as each child takes their turn to swim. Ask each child to mime finding a treasure chest at the bottom of the ocean. Taking turns, ask the children to share with the group what treasure they found in the chest.

5. Invite the children to build a story about something they saw under the sea. Begin by recapping the ideas the children created in the earlier activities by saying: "Who can remember all the things we saw under the sea?" Jo saw a mermaid. "Tyab saw seaweed and a crab." "Some children saw fish and others saw a shipwreck." "Who could the main character in our story be?"

6. Ask open questions to find out more about the main character: "What's their name?" "How old are they?" "Can you describe what they look like?" "Who are their friends?" "Where do they live?" "What do they enjoy?" "What do they dislike?"

Ask open questions to find out what problem the main character may need to resolve in the story: "How do they feel today?" "Why?" "What do they want?" "What is stopping them getting this?" "Why?" Begin telling the story using the children's ideas. Ask the children to give you describing words to help you tell the story related to the topic. For this topic you could use: ripples, waves, salty, cold, gurgling, bubbles, whoosh, splash. Ask open questions to find out how the children think the problem can be solved: "What might help them?" "Do they need to ask for help?" "Who from?" "Where from?" "What happens next?" "How do you think we can end our story?" "Is it a happy ending?"

). Retell the story including the ending.

And another idea:

▶ There are many good story and information books available to help introduce an underwater topic e.g. Tiddler by Julia Donaldson, Rainbow Fish by Marcus Pfister and Commotion in the Ocean by Giles Andreae.

▶ Make submarines from cardboard boxes. Cut out port-holes and attach cardboard tubes to represent the periscope. Invite children to decorate their very own submarine with scraps of cloth, lace, trim, pom-poms, glitter glue, ribbon, paint or felt-tip pens. Place the children's submarines onto the blue cloth and build a submarine story.

▶ Create an underwater role-play area. Hang streamers from the ceiling to represent seaweed, decorate a builder's tray with sand, pebbles and shells and fill jars with a mixture of water and blue or green food colouring. Props to include in the dressing up box are goggles, snorkelling masks, swimsuits, flippers and armbands, as well as small world sea creatures and fish.

Storybuilding worlds – Outer space

This activity is a good introduction to the topic of space travel. Role-play and drama are included to get children acting out the stories they make up and bring them to life.

Group size: 3-8 children; larger groups.

What you need:

▶ a roll of tin foil for space helmets

▶ a cloth bag or fishing net for 'gathering' story facts (optional)

What you do:

- Explain to the children that you are going on a journey into space.

- Suggest that the children put on astronaut helmets before you set off on the journey. This helps children to get into character and really feel like they are going on a journey into space. Simply wrapping and scrunching tinfoil into a hat shape on each child's head is all you need.

- Tell the children: "It's time to take off now so let's count down from 10 to 1." All shout together 'Blast Off!' Ask the children to make rocket noises and make movements until you shout "Freeze" to stop all action.

- Sit the children down and ask them to pretend they are astronauts inside a rocket. Suggest that you can see the moon ahead and you need their help to steer the rocket so that it can land on the moon. Invite children to take turns to walk outside of the rocket on the surface of the moon, and bring something back to the rocket that they have found. This may be: a star, an alien, moonrock, mooncheese, moondust, a moon mouse, the man on the moon, etc. Put all the imaginary objects into a bag or a story collecting net (fishing net) and tell the children it's time to fly back to earth so you can start building your story.

- Begin by unpacking all the facts you collected to find a character for your story: "Who can remember all the things we've seen in space today?" "Did we find any characters for our story? An alien? A star? The man on the moon?" "Who could the main character in our story be?"

- Ask open questions to find out more about the main character: "What is their name?" "How old are they?" "Can you describe what they look like?" "Who are their friends?" "Where do they live?" "What do they enjoy?" "What do they dislike?"

- Ask open questions to find out what problem the main character may need to resolve in the story: "How do they feel today?" "Why?" "What do they want?" "What is stopping them getting this?" "Why?"

- Begin telling the story, using the children's ideas. Ask the children to give you describing words to help you tell the story related to the topic. For outer space you may use: Whoosh, bang, sparkle, float, zoom, dark, silver, etc.

- Ask open questions to find out how the children think the problem in the story can be solved: "What might help the character?" "Do they need to ask for help?" "Who from?" "Where from?" "What happens next?" "How do you think we can end our story?" "Is it a happy ending?"

10. Retell the story including the ending.

And another idea:

▶ Create a topic book box including information books on space and stories such as How to Catch a Star by Oilver Jeffers and Aliens Love Underpants by Claire Freedman.

▶ Using large cardboard boxes, build a space rocket in your outdoor area. Cut boxes open vertically, open them up and join with other boxes, or curve them around so that they lean against a wall. Make control panels using old computer keyboards or simply by adding bottle tops or sticking the plastic trays inside chocolate boxes to cereal boxes.

▶ Create a solar system out of papier-mâché balloons. Learn about the sizes of the planets and try to use larger balloons to represent larger planets. The planets can be hung inside your classroom near to your role-play area, or under a shelter in your outdoor area. Children will enjoy using large construction materials to build rockets and space pods to journey into space!

Storybuilding worlds – A forest house

This activity will transform your pop-up tent or den into a story space, which will encourage children to see story making spaces all over your setting, rather than restricting Storybuilding to one particular area. Different areas will offer new experiences for children's senses, which in turn will influence their imaginative thinking.

In this activity, the children will accompany you to an imaginary house in the forest for tea and a story.

Group size: 3-6 children. However, it can be modified for larger groups if you are an experienced Storybuilder.

What you need:

I will need

▶ a pop-up tent or den

▶ pictures of forest landscapes, and of the animals and people you might find in the forest

▶ a CD of evocative music or forest sounds (optional)

▶ a choice of costume such as an apron or hat for you to get into character (optional)

▶ a Storybuilding bag full of forest themed objects such as leaves, twigs, soft toys or puppets of woodland creatures, acorns, conkers, small stones and rocks, a feather, moss, etc.

What you do:

1. Look at pictures of forests gathered from magazines and the Internet and talk about forest environments. "What would you see if you went on a walk through the forest?" "What kind of plants/animals might you see in a forest?" "What else might you see/hear/ smell?"

2. Invite children to take an imaginary walk with you through the forest. You could ask the children to lie down, close their eyes and use their imaginations to explore the forest. It will help if you use evocative music or verbally guide them

3. Suggest to the children that they have come across a little house in the forest. Invite the children to mime knocking at the door then peering through the keyhole: "What did you see when you looked through the keyhole?" "What kind of person or animal might live in this house?"

4. Invite the children to meet the person or animal that lives in this house. Ask open questions to find out more about the person or animal they have chosen as the occupant: "What is their name?" "How many people or animals live here?" "How do they feel today?" "Why?"

5. If your den or tent is big enough, invite the children to enter the 'house in the forest'. If not, then it is fine to pretend you are all inside. Get in role as the person or animal that lives in the house and mime making tea for the children You may find an apron, a hat or another piece of costume helps you get into character more.

6. Use the Storybuilding bag of forest objects, for your forest story. You may wish to follow the method described in Storybuilding bags by theme.

After the story has finished tell the children it is getting dark and they need to make their way home. They can lie down again and imagine their walk out of the forest.

Encourage the children to return to the forest house in their free play.

And another idea:

▶ Read Hansel and Gretel, Goldilocks and the Three Bears, Russian Fairytales or The Snow Maiden story. Display these books invitingly along with the Storybuilding bag, or position them beside your den or tent for the children to use in their free play.

▶ Make gingerbread and use cookie cutters to cut it into stars and trees. Decorate with icing and other edible treats.

Making a story den

Den Storybuilding is a particularly valuable activity for children with autism and other additional needs because the space feels safe and manageable and the story thread can be easier to follow when external distractions are at a minimum

There are many ways to encourage children to experiment with den making using a wide range of materials. Cardboard boxes can help children to explore making forts, but simply hanging sheets over washing lines can make a useful hidden space for children's play activities. In this activity we are going to look at how to make a Tipi den.

Group size: 2-4 children

What you need:

8-10 long poles such as bamboo or broom handles (around 6 feet tall)

2-3 blankets, throws, sheets or a tarpaulin to wrap around the wood.

a ball of strong string and a pair of sharp scissors (adult use only)

What you do:

Find a piece of earthy ground that allows you to push the wooden poles easily into the soil.

Push the poles into the ground in a circle and cross the poles at the top to form a tipi style top. Make sure you leave a large enough gap between two of the poles for your den entrance.

Tie the string around the crossed tops to secure them together. Gaffa tape would also work. Test the structure carefully to ensure it is safe.

Cover the Tipi with a sheet or a throw. You can peg back the sheet at the entrance so the children can find their way inside.

Invite the children inside to build a story with you.

And another idea:

▶ You could plant runner beans around the base of the den. As the vines grow, wrap them around the poles to create a living den. This also works with scented vines such as honeysuckle.

▶ Dens are a great place to experiment with light and dark. If you cover parts of the den with lace or chiffon, the light will change inside. You can also experiment with shining torches at the den to see how the fabric absorbs light or use thick fabric to create a total blackout. This is great for creating atmosphere in stories.

▶ Read We're Going on a Bear Hunt by Michael Rosen and create an outdoor Bear Hunt trail that leads to the Tipi den. March along the trail chanting and miming the story, and huddle together in the den pretending to be in the bear's cave. If space permits, create a second 'home' den where children can hide under the bedclothes when you reach the end of the story!

Rebuilding popular stories

Another useful way for children to explore how stories are put together is to ask children to consider what happened before a favourite story started or what might happen to the characters after the book is finished. You can also suggest they look at a story from the point of view of another character. Pulling stories apart like this offers so many opportunities to play with stories and make them your own. Here is an example of how you could rebuild the popular story The Tiger Who Came to Tea by Judith Kerr.

Group size: 6-8 children

What you need:

a copy of The Tiger Who Came to Tea by Judith Kerr

a variety of food packets the children have brought in from home

What you do:

Before the Storybuilding session, ask the children to bring in food packets from home. Ask parents/carers to help the children gather clean packaging from their favourite foods as well as any traditional or cultural foods that the families eat at home.

If the children are not familiar with The Tiger Who Came to Tea, begin the session by reading through the story. Look at illustrations from the book and help the children to recall the events in the story.

Invite the children to show the food packets they have brought from home. Encourage them to pretend to take food out of the package: "What is that food called?" "When do you normally eat this food?" (morning, dinnertime, for a cultural celebration etc). Display the food packages nearby.

Invite the children to build a story with you about what the Tiger did after he left Sophie's house. Ask questions: "Where will the Tiger visit next?" "Where do you think the Tiger might visit somewhere near to school/nursery?" "I wonder what the Tiger would like to eat next?" "Is he looking for another meal?" "Do the people here feed the Tiger like Sophie's mum?" "How do they feel when they see the Tiger?" "Does the Tiger cause any trouble here?" "How does the Tiger feel?"

Begin telling the story using the children's ideas. Ask the children to give you descriptive words about where the Tiger visits and how he feels there. (Some words to explore are: starving, greedy, mischievous, hungry, peckish.)

Ask the children what food the Tiger eats next. Invite each child to pick a food packet from the display and place it in a line in the middle of the circle. Together with the children, point to the packages and recall all the foods the Tiger ate.

Ask the children how the Tiger feels after eating all that food, is it time for the Tiger to go home? Is he tired? Or does he want to go somewhere else?

Retell the story and invite the children to help you recall every food the Tiger ate using the food packets as prompts. End the story with a concluding line from the book.

And another idea:

▶ Look at a range of restaurant and take-away menus or supermarket recipe cards and magazines. Talk about the different kinds of meals you can orde Help the children to make a menu of the Tiger's favourite foods. They can draw pictures or cut out and stick images.

▶ Learn about what happens when you visit a shop. If convenient, arrange to go on a walk to a local grocery shop or supermarket and encourage the children to look around them and tell you what they can see, e.g. shelves, types of food and drink, a cashier, cash registers etc. The children will benefit from watching you buy an item of food and listening to the kinds of language we use in shops.

▶ Set up your role-play corner with a variety of food packets, shopping bags purses and money. If you have a role-play cash register then use it or a decorated cardboard box would do. Encourage children to role-play a shopping trip to the supermarket to buy food for a big dinner or celebratio to which the Tiger has been invited.

The Little Books Club

There is always something in Little Books to help and inspire you.
Packed full of lovely ideas, Little Books meet the need for exciting and
practical activities that are fun to do, address the Early Learning Goals
and can be followed in most settings. Everyone is a winner!

We publish 5 new Little Books a year. Little Books Club members receive
each of these 5 books as soon as they are published for a reduced price.
The subscription cost is £29.99 – a one off payment that buys
the 5 new books for £4.99 instead of £8.99 each.

In addition to this, Little Books Club Members receive:
· Free postage and packing on anything ordered from the
  Featherstone catalogue
· A 15% discount voucher upon joining which can be used to buy any
  number of books from the Featherstone catalogue
· Members price of £4.99 on any additional Little Book purchased
· A regular, free newsletter dealing with club news, special offers and
  aspects of Early Years curriculum and practice
· All new Little Books on approval - return in good condition within 30
  days and we'll refund the cost to your club account

Call 020 7758 0200 or email: littlebooks@bloomsbury.com for
an enrolment pack. Or download an application form from our website:
www.acblack.com/featherstone

The Little Books series consists of:

All Through the Year

Bags, Boxes & Trays

Big Projects

Bricks and Boxes

Celebrations

Christmas

Circle Time

Clay and Malleable
Materials

Clothes and Fabrics

Colour, Shape and Number

Cooking from Stories

Cooking Together

Counting

Dance

Dance, with music CD

Discovery Bottles

Dough

Drama from Stories

50

Explorations

Fine Motor Skills

Fun on a Shoestring

Games with Sounds

Growing Things

ICT

Investigations

Junk Music

Kitchen Stuff

Language Fun

Light and Shadow

Listening

Living Things

Look and Listen

Making Books and Cards

Maps and Plans

Making Poetry

Mark Making

Maths Activities

Maths from Stories

Maths Outdoors

Maths Songs and Games

Messy Play

Minibeast Hotels

Multi-Sensory Stories

Music

Nursery Rhymes

Opposites

Outdoor Play

Outside in All Weathers

Parachute Play

Persona Dolls

Phonics

Playground Games

Prop Boxes for Role Play

Props for Writing

Puppet Making

Puppets in Stories

Resistant Materials

Role Play

Sand and Water

Science through Art

Scissor Skills

Sewing and Weaving

Sequencing Skills

Small World Play

Sound Ideas

Special Days

Stories from around
World

Storyboards

Storybuilding

Storytelling

Seasons

Time and Money

Time and Place

Traditional Tales

Treasure Baskets

Treasureboxes

Tuff Spot Activities

Washing Lines

Woodwork

Writing

All available from
www.bloomsbury.com